Remarkable
LATERAL
THINKING
PUZZLES

Remarkable LATERAL THINKING PUZZLES

Paul Sloane & Des MacHale

**PUZZLE
WRIGHT
PRESS**

New York

PUZZLE
WRIGHT
PRESS
New York

An Imprint of Sterling Publishing
387 Park Avenue South
New York, NY 10016

Puzzlewright Press and the distinctive Puzzlewright Press logo are
registered trademarks of Sterling Publishing Co., Inc.

© 2014 by Paul Sloane and Des MacHale

ISBN 978-1-4549-0989-7

Distributed in Canada by Sterling Publishing
℅ Canadian Manda Group, 165 Dufferin Street
Toronto, Ontario, Canada M6K 3H6
Distributed in the United Kingdom by GMC Distribution Services
Castle Place, 166 High Street, Lewes, East Sussex, England BN7 1XU
Distributed in Australia by Capricorn Link (Australia) Pty. Ltd.
P.O. Box 704, Windsor, NSW 2756, Australia

For information about custom editions, special sales, and premium and
corporate purchases, please contact Sterling Special Sales at 800-805-5489 or
specialsales@sterlingpublishing.com.

Manufactured in the United States of America

2 4 6 8 10 9 7 5 3 1

www.puzzlewright.com

Contents

Introduction

Each of the puzzles in this book is a strange situation with an unexpected explanation. They are designed as a form of game for a small group, where one person knows the answer and the others try to figure it out by asking questions, which can be answered only with "yes," "no," or "irrelevant." The questioners will need to think laterally and come at the problem from different directions.

You can play the game right away by picking any puzzle in the book and peeking at the answer, or you can try solving on your own first, using the clues provided in the middle section of the book (which you can also use during the group game if players get stuck) ... but, of course, the best resource is always your own imagination.

Although all the puzzles are solved the same way, the book is divided into two sections: Lateral Situations and Lateral Factuals. The difference between them is that while they both feature improbable-seeming situations and explanations, the Lateral Factuals all concern real (if unusual) occurrences. We certainly don't expect people to know the strange facts in these puzzles, but that's what makes them ideal for the game!

Special thanks to Tara Curry for "Unbreakable" and Myrna Smith for "Changing Clothes."

—Paul Sloane and Des MacHale

LATERAL SITUATIONS

Instruction for Destruction

· ·

A man gave a simple instruction for a car that resulted in ruin for a computer. How?

Clues on p. 45/Answer on p. 72

Blind Dates

· ·

What do these four dates have in common?

    A.   2nd of May
    B.   7th of September
    C.   4th of March
    D.   1st of December

Clues on p. 45/Answer on p. 72

Fire Escape

A frail elderly woman was asleep in the bedroom of her house when a fire started in her kitchen. The fire quickly spread and soon the only stairway in the house was ablaze. The woman woke up and knew that she could not open any of the windows. The stairway was impassable and she could not climb onto the roof. How did she escape?

Clues on p. 45/Answer on p. 72

Phew!

A company that sold its main product to consumers decided to add something foul-smelling to the product. Why did they do this?

Clues on p. 45/Answer on p. 72

A Cold Reception

A man hired a new young assistant for his business in January. The premises were surrounded by ice and snow so he gave the assistant the job of clearing all the paths to make them safe for customers. The assistant did this quickly and efficiently but the man immediately fired him. Why?

Clues on p. 46/Answer on p. 72

Bad Spelling

A man is hired to carve a certain number in numerals. Instead, he carves it in letters (e.g., "thirty-five" instead of "35"). He is immediately arrested. Why?

Clues on p. 46/Answer on p. 72

Green-Collar Crime

A tree grew in the exact spot where Steve committed a crime. What was the crime?

Clues on p. 46/Answer on p. 72

Take That

Give a man one and he will thank you for a long time; give him two, and he will hate you, but maybe not for long. What are we talking about?

Clues on p. 46/Answer on p. 73

Traveling Bags

A frequent business traveler's luggage often arrives in the wrong city—much more often, in fact, than for any of his coworkers, all of whom travel as much as he does, with the same airline. Why?

Clues on p. 47/Answer on p. 73

The Landslide

A man was traveling by bus on a very dangerous road in the South American Andes. He got off the bus to do some exploration but after a few minutes, to his horror, there was a landslide and the bus was entirely engulfed and everyone on board was killed. The man screamed and shouted, "I wish I hadn't gotten off that bus." Why on earth did he say that?

Clues on p. 47/Answer on p. 73

Unbreakable

A valuable object fell to the floor but did not break. People were disappointed. Why?

Clues on p. 47/Answer on p. 73

A Fishy Story

A woman wanted to buy something so she put some raw fish into her handbag. Why?

Clues on p. 47/Answer on p. 73

Dog Days

Betty did not like her neighbor Ethel, so she got a dog in order to annoy her. The dog was quiet and good-natured, so why was the neighbor annoyed?

Clues on p. 48/Answer on p. 73

Bungling and Burgling

How was a bungling thief able to walk free despite leaving his DNA at the crime scene, being caught on a security camera, and the police tracking him down to his home?

Clues on p. 48/Answer on p. 73

Well-Suited

Andy, Ben, and Charlie share an interest. Andy and Ben are wearing open-neck shirts and jeans. Charlie has a black suit. Consequently Charlie is given $100,000. Andy and Ben are unhappy. What is going on?

Clues on p. 48/Answer on p. 74

Razed to New Heights

For many years people wanted to have it knocked down, but when it was knocked down, another one had to be built to protect it. What was it?

Clues on p. 48/Answer on p. 74

Poor Sed

From birth, Sed was a member of a minority constituting about 1% of the human race. For about sixty years, people teased him about it, but over a period of about ten years he ceased to be a member of that minority. What are we talking about?

Clues on p. 49/Answer on p. 74

Lost Sheep

A shepherd went out into the wilderness in search of one lost sheep, rather than looking after the 99 that had returned. Why did he do this?

Clues on p. 49/Answer on p. 74

Low Visibility

John and George stood in a field facing each other from 50 yards apart. Both men had excellent eyesight and neither was wearing anything on his head. John could see George but George could not see John. Why?

Clues on p. 49/Answer on p. 74

Changing Clothes

After Anna's husband died she replaced some of her wardrobe. Why?

Clues on p. 49/Answer on p. 75

A Big Leap

The airplane was at an altitude of 15,000 feet when Andy leapt out. He had no parachute. He fell through the air and landed on hard ground. Jarred but unscathed he walked away. How come?

Clues on p. 50/Answer on p. 75

Visiting Rights

A couple bought something they liked. They did not keep it in their home but went to see it once or twice a year. What was it?

Clues on p. 50/Answer on p. 75

Lead Astray

. . . .

One team took the lead and then the other team took the lead from them. The first team got the lead back. Both teams were arrested. Why?

Clues on p. 50/Answer on p. 75

The Long Bath

. . . .

Ivan had spent all day outdoors so when he came home he ran a bath. He did not get into the bath and he let the water out five days later. Why?

Clues on p. 50/Answer on p. 75

Watch Out!

. . . .

Which popular food can harm or even kill people, even if those people are not allergic to it and do not choke on it?

Clues on p. 50/Answer on p. 76

That's Bazaar

The priest did something to deter crime. His action also increased sales at the church bazaar. What did he do?

Clues on p. 51/Answer on p. 76

Double Trouble

They come in two parts. Parents often buy them for their children, but sometimes children buy them for their parents. What are they?

Clues on p. 51/Answer on p. 76

The Weak Bridge

• •

Two cities, A and B, are 200 miles apart. A truck weighing three tons and one pound (including the driver's weight and the truck's entire load), is driven from A to B. Near B is a single-lane bridge that the truck must cross. The bridge will collapse if it has to bear any load of more than three tons. How does the driver get his truck and load safely across?

Clues on p. 51/Answer on p. 76

Self-Fulfilling Prophecy

• •

What sports situation might cause itself to happen in a more literal sense to certain fans?

Clues on p. 51/Answer on p. 76

Commuter Bug

A group of people were happy but I wasn't, because I was late for work. What was happening?

Clues on p. 52/Answer on p. 76

Just Trying to Blend In

Why might a chameleon make a good soccer linesman?

Clues on p. 52/Answer on p. 76

Queasy Rider

What can an adult do to prevent carsickness that a child cannot?

Clues on p. 52/Answer on p. 77

Bad Move

Why did a greedy man move from his large house in a prosperous area to a small house in a rough neighborhood?

Clues on p. 52/Answer on p. 77

Less Money, Please!

Why would workers go on strike because they wanted to make less money?

Clues on p. 53/Answer on p. 77

Two Jackets Required

Why did a businessman buy a suit with two jackets and one pair of trousers?

Clues on p. 53/Answer on p. 78

Bad Habits

Two monks had sinned and confessed their sins. Each was given the penance of walking five miles with a dried pea in his shoe. They each received a dried pea and took their walks together. After returning to the monastery, the first monk's foot was sore and blistered, but the second, even after walking five miles wearing a shoe with a pea in it, was completely unscathed. How did he avoid injury?

Clues on p. 53/Answer on p. 78

Brother or Sister

Kelly was a little girl who was diagnosed with a deadly disease. Doctors advised her parents that the only cure was a bone marrow transplant from a brother or sister, and it was needed within one month. Kelly was an only child. Her parents had never had any other children and her mother was not pregnant. How was Kelly saved?

Clues on p. 53/Answer on p. 78

Impressive Identification

When Tony arrived at the soccer match he saw that there were about 30 people watching the game. He had been told that John, the father of one of the players, would be there. Tony had never met John before and had never seen a picture of him but he walked up to a man and said, "Are you John?" "Yes," was the reply. How had Tony known?

Clues on p. 54/Answer on p. 78

On Reflection, It Makes Sense

Why did a man buy a car with the European license plate number 800808 AHM?

Clues on p. 54/Answer on p. 78

Pen Name

Why did an aspiring young author optimistically change his first name from Brian to Bryan?

Clues on p. 54/Answer on p. 78

Dress to Impress

Why did a group of thieves dress so smartly?

Clues on p. 54/Answer on p. 79

Shaven Head 1

Why did a woman shave a number onto her son's head?

Clues on p. 55/Answer on p. 80

Shaven Head 2

Why did a student completely shave his head?

Clues on p. 55/Answer on p. 80

The Reluctant Smoker

A man who disliked smoking lit a cigarette in order to reach his goal more quickly. How did it help?

Clues on p. 55/Answer on p. 80

Going Full Circle

Why did a woman take a circular disk with her when she went shopping?

Clues on p. 55/Answer on p. 80

Off With Its Head

What loses its head every morning but gets it back every evening?

Clues on p. 55/Answer on p. 80

That's Cold

A man was driving his children to visit Santa Claus but took a wrong turn. He wound up near the coldest place in the universe. How come?

Clues on p. 56/Answer on p. 80

This Place Is a Zoo

Why does a man who works in a zoo write a capital letter B and a capital letter D on the back of his hand?

Clues on p. 56/Answer on p. 81

Bagman

Why is a man carrying the following items in a bag—a lemon, a bottle of milk, and a clothes iron?

Clues on p. 56/Answer on p. 81

100% Chance of Robbery

They were robbed because the weather changed. What happened?

Clues on p. 56/Answer on p. 81

LATERAL
FACTUALS

Getaway Route

A crocodile can run faster than a human, so what should you do if you are being chased by a crocodile on flat ground with no trees or other obstacles?

Clues on p. 57/Answer on p. 81

Wedged In

A famous man slept as a boy with wooden wedges between his fingers. Why?

Clues on p. 57/Answer on p. 81

Don't Stand So Close to Me

A man was embarrassed at work because he sometimes had to stand very close to women. What did he invent that is in common use today?

Clues on p. 57/Answer on p. 82

Train Fare

A train in Peru travels through spectacular scenery. What unusual item is available for passengers' refreshment?

Clues on p. 57/Answer on p. 82

There's an Awful Lot of Coffee in Brazil

Brazil produces a huge amount of coffee beans each year. When the coffee quota has been met, what use is made of the surplus?

Clues on p. 58/Answer on p. 82

Bright Idea

Bulls are known to be color-blind. Why then do matadors wear brightly colored cloaks?

Clues on p. 58/Answer on p. 82

Up the Spout

Can you find a connection between *Moby-Dick* and coffee?

Clues on p. 58/Answer on p. 82

Men Only

Exactly twelve men have done this so far, but no woman. What is it?

Clues on p. 58/Answer on p. 83

Mighty Mini

He sounds royal, was just eighteen inches tall, and scared a lot of people. Who was he?

Clues on p. 59/Answer on p. 83

Dangerous Days

During the period from February 23 to February 25, 2008, five people in Samara, Russia, all died of the same cause. What was it?

Clues on p. 59/Answer on p. 83

No Birds Allowed

Many creatures, from insects to monkeys, have been sent into space. Why have birds never been sent into space?

Clues on p. 59/Answer on p. 83

A Handful

From ancient times until a few hundred years ago we knew only six, but that number was later increased to nine, until recently being reduced to eight. What are we talking about?

Clues on p. 59/Answer on p. 83

Happy Families

Family-run firms that are passed down from generation to generation generally perform less well than firms where the CEO is chosen by the board. However, this is not the case in Japan, where family firms do better than in most other countries. Why?

Clues on p. 59/Answer on p. 84

The Prank

How did a prankster use a pile of old tires to cause mass panic in the town of Sitka, Alaska, on April 1, 1974?

Clues on p. 60/Answer on p. 84

Beat to Death

How were 226 men killed by a rhythm in 1850?

Clues on p. 60/Answer on p. 84

South Pole Position

Is it probable or improbable that the continent of Antarctica was once situated in the tropical regions of the earth, and how can we tell?

Clues on p. 60/Answer on p. 84

Sales Boom

According to *The Independent* of London, what is thought to have led to a 700% increase in the sale of pencils in 2006?

Clues on p. 60/Answer on p. 84

26 Years

It happened in 2013, but the last time it happened before that was in 1987. What is it?

Clues on p. 60/Answer on p. 84

A Mysterious Woman

One woman has banknotes that are worth more than other people's banknotes. Who is she?

Clues on p. 61/Answer on p. 84

Thanks but No Thanks

. . . .

The houses in a village had all been painted white once. A company offered to paint them white again for free but the offer was refused. Why?

Clues on p. 61/Answer on p. 85

Guess Your Weight

. . . .

To the nearest million tons, what is the weight of the Earth?

Clues on p. 61/Answer on p. 85

Rich Cooking

A food service worker was illiterate—but, because of this, came into possession of some very valuable items. How come?

Clues on p. 61/Answer on p. 86

Delayed Effect

There were no terrorist attacks in the U.S. in the ten years after 9/11 but many more Americans died as a result of the terrorists' actions. How?

Clues on p. 62/Answer on p. 86

Solve for X

Only one X has won an X. What is X?

Clues on p. 62/Answer on p. 86

Danger in the Garden

In terms of the number of accidents it causes, the lawnmower is the most dangerous gardening item. What do you think is the second most dangerous?

Clues on p. 62/Answer on p. 86

Phony Baloney

Why did a man named Alfonso Nino get a number of angry phone calls blaming him for something that was obviously not his fault?

Clues on p. 62/Answer on p. 87

The Deadly Bite
. . . .

The teeth of the dead can still cause harm. How?

Clues on p. 62/Answer on p. 87

Not Enough
. . . .

Its name implies that it will have 1,000, but the maximum in reality is more like 750. What are we talking about?

Clues on p. 63/Answer on p. 87

Par for the Course
. . . .

In a golf tournament several players recorded a score of par but only one golfer had "PAR" written after his name. How come?

Clues on p. 63/Answer on p. 87

Does Not Compute

. . . .

They go from having 22 to having 32 of one item, but also from having 350 of another item to having 209. What are they?

Clues on p. 63/Answer on p. 88

What Was That?

. . . .

What big event resulted in deafness, lower temperatures, and beautiful sunsets?

Clues on p. 63/Answer on p. 88

A Grave Problem

. . . .

What person's remains lie in the remotest grave of all time?

Clues on p. 64/Answer on p. 88

Quo Vadis?

· ·

What did the ancient Romans do that still troubles gardeners in Britain today?

Clues on p. 64/Answer on p. 89

When Push Comes to Shove

· ·

What is moved about eleven yards every New Year's Day?

Clues on p. 64/Answer on p. 89

Super-Efficient

· ·

What is the most efficient method of light production (i.e., that which produces the greatest amount of light for the smallest expenditure of energy)?

Clues on p. 64/Answer on p. 89

Country Cousins

· ·

What do the countries Malawi, Cyprus, Ireland, Pakistan, and Japan have in common?

Clues on p. 65/Answer on p. 89

Unseen

· ·

What very common substance has never been seen in person by over half of the world's population?

Clues on p. 65/Answer on p. 89

Getting Overly Personal

Why do total strangers regularly send their own genetic material to each other?

Clues on p. 65/Answer on p. 90

Tee Shot

Who was the American golfer whose long drive helped Europe to victory in the 2012 Ryder Cup?

Clues on p. 65/Answer on p. 90

Cover Charge

What was the original function of tablecloths?

Clues on p. 66/Answer on p. 90

Big Al
. . . .

When Al was taken out of a big country, it became a much smaller country. Why?

Clues on p. 66/Answer on p. 90

Look Both Ways
. . . .

What group has taken turns looking one way, then the other, for many years?

Clues on p. 66/Answer on p. 90

Poor Reflection
. . . .

Why do Parisian criminals on scooters bump into the side-view mirrors of cars?

Clues on p. 66/Answer on p. 91

Mint Condition

Why are the edges of some coins milled?

Clues on p. 67/Answer on p. 91

The Hunters

Some hunters make money by tracking a certain marsupial, which they never catch or want to catch or even see. What do they do?

Clues on p. 67/Answer on p. 91

Swap Shop

Why does China lead the world in the frequency of human transplant surgery?

Clues on p. 67/Answer on p. 92

Right This Way

Why does my hotel room have an extra floor covering and an arrow on the ceiling?

Clues on p. 67/Answer on p. 92

Devious!

Without its small deviation it would probably be unknown, but it is world famous. What is it?

Clues on p. 68/Answer on p. 92

Stage Fright
. . . .

Why was Shakespeare's play *King Lear* banned in England for 10 years?

Clues on p. 68/Answer on p. 93

Sweet!
. . . .

You often see sugar in action movies. Why?

Clues on p. 68/Answer on p. 93

Who Was That Masked Man?
. . . .

A woman gave a coin to a masked man. She had never met him before and he was not a criminal. Who was he?

Clues on p. 68/Answer on p. 93

Deal or No Deal?
· ·

How did winning a suitcase turn René into a millionaire?

Clues on p. 69/Answer on p. 93

Breaking the Habit
· ·

What unusual plan did a psychologist put forward to reduce drug abuse?

Clues on p. 69/Answer on p. 93

The Other Leg
· ·

Why did a businesswoman have one brown leg and one white one?

Clues on p. 69/Answer on p. 93

Hand in Glove

Why did a girl go to a tennis match wearing a long leather glove?

Clues on p. 69/Answer on p. 94

Detection

The first time they tried this test, 5,000 passed and none failed. But the police still found the killer. How?

Clues on p. 70/Answer on p. 95

Most Unlucky

Hans held a world record and unfortunately died because of it. How?

Clues on p. 70/Answer on p. 95

Born to Be Wild

History records that Gorgias of Epirus was born in unique circumstances. What were they?

Clues on p. 70/Answer on p. 95

Fulfillment

It was built, it was filled, it was used. Over 100 years later it is still full but it is no longer used. What is it?

Clues on p. 70/Answer on p. 95

CLUES

Instruction for Destruction

- It was a very cold day.
- The man received a text message from his wife asking for help.
- He misunderstood her message and gave the solution for a different problem.

Blind Dates

- This has nothing to do with historical events.
- Read the question literally.
- Look for a pattern.

Fire Escape

- She escaped without using the stairway.
- She walked out of the house.
- Be careful you're not making incorrect assumptions about the layout of the house.

Phew!

- This was done for reasons of safety.
- Consumers consumed this product but did not eat or drink it.
- The smell helped you notice the product.

A Cold Reception

- You need to determine what kind of business he worked in.

- The young man took some initiative to improve safety in the icy conditions.

- His business afforded him access to something commonly used to melt snow, although the type that he had available is not generally considered appropriate for that purpose.

- His actions saved some customers from slipping but upset other customers a great deal.

Bad Spelling

- He was not sending a message.

- He was arrested for theft.

- He had chosen to use letters rather than numbers for his personal gain.

- Find out what he was carving.

Green-Collar Crime

- It was a minor offense.

- The tree is relevant to the crime.

- The tree resulted from the crime.

Take That

- We are talking about a man in a particular unpleasant circumstance.

- Give him one and it will help him, but two will definitely not.

- The circumstance is a dangerous one, and giving a man one might save his life.

Traveling Bags

- The unlucky traveler does something differently from all of his coworkers, but it has nothing to do with how he prepares his luggage.
- He always checks his bags at the counter, with the assistance of an airline worker.
- He has a very short temper.

The Landslide

- He was genuinely aghast that the bus and its passengers had been swept away.
- He did not wish that he had died with them.
- He regretted his actions.

Unbreakable

- It was not an accident that the object fell.
- Many people were celebrating.
- A couple was involved.

A Fishy Story

- She was acting in a very devious way.
- She was intending to make a major purchase.
- She wanted to buy the item for a good price.

Dog Days

- Betty and Ethel lived close to each other so Ethel could see and hear Betty and her dog next door.

- The dog did not do anything that was annoying. It was clean, quiet, and tidy.

- Betty used the dog to annoy Ethel but not by the dog's actions or appearance.

Bungling and Burgling

- The nature of the crime is not important for solving the puzzle.

- The criminal was arrested. The police matched his DNA to that found at the crime scene and an eyewitness identified him.

- He had no alibi, made no plea-bargain, and there was no external pressure on the police or corruption involved.

- There was something very unusual about this particular criminal that meant that it could not be proved that he had committed the crime.

Well-Suited

- Charlie walked away with $100,000, flushed with success.

- His gain was not the result of his clothing.

- The statements in the puzzle are true but misleading.

- They sat at a table.

Razed to New Heights

- It was famous.

- It was in Western Europe, and you can still see parts of it.

- It kept people apart and caused people to die.

Poor Sed

- Sed suffered because of something he had.
- He lost it after many years.
- People made fun of him because of he was part of a minority.
- Very few of this minority are found in Africa or Asia.

Lost Sheep

- He neglected 99 to search for one lost sheep but he had a rational reason for this.
- He was concerned about the long-term health of the herd.
- There was something different about the sheep that was lost.

Low Visibility

- The light was good.
- No mirrors, reflections, or unnatural obstacles were involved.
- As they faced each other both men were capable of seeing the other but only one did.

Changing Clothes

- She disposed of clothes that she would not wear now that she lived alone.
- This has nothing to do with the color of the items.
- The clothes she replaced were mainly dresses and blouses.
- She did not do this for financial gain but for convenience.

A Big Leap

- The plane was 15,000 feet above sea level.

- Andy had no special equipment, special skill, or special clothing.

- Andy's fall was not cushioned in any way. He touched nothing on his way down until he hit the hard ground.

Visiting Rights

- They kept it in another building.

- It was valuable.

- They liked to see it.

Lead Astray

- The teams were competing but not in a sport.

- Check all your assumptions here very carefully or you might be misled.

- This puzzle would not work if it were read aloud.

The Long Bath

- Ivan filled the bath with cold water.

- The activity he was engaged in while he was outdoors is important.

- He used the bath to clean something.

Watch Out!

- This food is not poisonous.

- People could be injured or killed by this food even before they have bought, prepared, or eaten it.

- It grows on trees.

That's Bazaar

- Thieves had stolen things from the church.

- The priest enlisted the help of some workers.

- This resulted in fewer robberies and more sales of jars of foodstuff at the church bazaar.

Double Trouble

- People who buy these items typically do so out of concern for the safety and well-being of others.

- When parents buy these, it is the parents who use them for the benefit of their children.

- These items can be used to aid awareness and communication.

The Weak Bridge

- The driver drove his truck safely across the bridge even though the bridge could only carry three tons.

- No buoyancy aids were used and the driver did not remove anything from the truck.

- If he had started his journey from B instead of A he might not have gotten across.

Self-Fulfilling Prophecy

- Some sports fans put their heart and soul into a game—and that can be stressful.

- The answer is a two-word term used to describe a dramatic conclusion to certain games.

Commuter Bug

- Not only were they happy, they were lucky and rich.
- I was left waiting.
- They had a ticket, and I also had a ticket.

Just Trying to Blend In

- Changing color is not the only special ability that chameleons have.
- A soccer linesman has to watch several aspects of the game.
- The chameleon can do something with its eyes that humans cannot.

Queasy Rider

- This does not involve medication, drugs, or treatment.
- How could you stay in a car but reduce the impact of carsickness?
- The unexpected twists and turns in a car can make you feel nauseous, so how can you make them less unexpected?

Bad Move

- He did this for financial gain.
- This does not involve buying or selling property of any kind, but he did spend a lot of money.
- People living in poor areas generally have worse expectations and outcomes in many areas, including education and health.

Less Money, Please!

- The workers literally wanted to make less money but they did not want to be worse off.

- Their strike was not about hours worked or workplace conditions or bonuses; the strikers just wanted to make less money.

- The managers of the business firmly resisted the workers' demands.

- They worked in a factory that made items of paper. (The same situation might occur in a factory making metal items.)

Two Jackets Required

- He bought the suit to wear to work.

- People at his office were expected to work very hard.

- He used the extra jacket to mislead people.

Bad Habits

- Nothing else was put in the shoe except a pea and a foot.

- Each monk put a pea in his shoe but one did something else first.

- What can you do with a pea?

Brother or Sister

- Kelly was an only child with no brothers or sisters alive or dead.

- Kelly's parents were both unusual in a similar respect.

- The doctors had advised that only a transplant from a brother or sister would do and a suitable one was found.

Impressive Identification

- Lots of parents and friends were there.

- John had no memorable distinguishing features and Tony did not recognize him from any previous description.

- John was not behaving any differently from any of the other spectators.

On Reflection, It Makes Sense

- There is a property of this set of letters and numbers that made the plate useful to the man.

- He was not a criminal. He was working in corporate communications.

- He wanted to use the image of the car in many different places.

Pen Name

- This has to do with writing, but not in the sense of writing books.

- He did this for convenience.

- He expected to have many fans.

Dress to Impress

- They planned to rob a place when there were no other people there.

- They dressed smartly so as to help avoid detection.

- They robbed a shop.

Shaven Head 1

- She did this to help others.
- There was nothing wrong with the boy but he was remarkable in one certain regard.
- The number was 4.

Shaven Head 2

- He was being deceitful.
- He wanted sympathy and mercy.
- He should have worked more and partied less.

The Reluctant Smoker

- He started to smoke in a place where smoking was forbidden.
- He was reprimanded but refused to stop smoking.
- He was pleased when sanctions were taken against him.

Going Full Circle

- She wanted to check something.
- She thought that the shops might try to deceive her.
- She bought clothes and liked to try them on.

Off With Its Head

- The answer is something that you know very well indeed.
- The answer can be found in your house, but it is not alive.
- You would find one in a hotel room, too.

That's Cold

- The man started his drive in Lapland.

- He arrived at a strange place that looks like a normal building.

- The place he visited can make things colder than they are on Pluto.

This Place Is a Zoo

- He wanted to remember something.

- The letters are initials of something for which the shape of each letter helps provide the mnemonic.

- He wanted to distinguish between two species of a type of animal.

Bagman

- Some people would consider this man a criminal but others would not.

- This would have happened before the days of electronic communication.

- He uses these items to help send and receive messages.

100% Chance of Robbery

- The victims were a couple who had gone away on vacation, during which their house was burgled.

- They left their cars in the driveway and lights were timed to come on in the house.

- Burglars could tell that the house was empty.

- They went on vacation to escape the cold.

Getaway Route

- There is a tactic you can use that makes it more difficult for the crocodile to catch you.

- It does not involve jumping or shouting and it works on flat ground.

- Think of a runner with the ball in football or soccer trying to evade tackles.

Wedged In

- He was a child prodigy.

- His parents wanted to help develop his skill.

- The wedges were designed to increase his reach.

- His first name was Frédéric.

Don't Stand So Close to Me

- He had an important job that involved examining people.

- What he invented was not an item of clothing but a piece of equipment.

- A certain profession uses this equipment, and you have very probably had it used on you.

Train Fare

- This item is not a food or a drink.

- The Peruvian trains travel through the Andes.

- Some people consume this item for their well-being.

There's an Awful Lot of Coffee in Brazil

- The excess coffee is not used as a food or drink product for humans or animals.

- It aids in transport ...

- ... but not in cars or buses, or in any vehicle that uses liquid fuel.

Bright Idea

- The matador's cloak is usually red but the bull cannot detect this color.

- This is not just tradition; there is a reason for the color.

- Bullfighting is very dangerous.

Up the Spout

- This is unrelated to flavors or types of coffee (or types of whales).

- It concerns a character in the book *Moby-Dick*.

- You have probably visited a place that is connected with this book.

Men Only

- This does not refer to something sports-related.

- There is no reason why a woman could not do this.

- Michael Jackson was not one of the 12 men but he did do something similar (in a sense).

Mighty Mini

- He looks much larger than 18 inches.

- He's a famous fictional character.

- He first appeared in 1933 (and had prominent reappearances in 1976 and 2005).

Dangerous Days

- These were unusual, violent, accidental deaths.

- Their deaths could only have happened in a very cold country, but they did not freeze to death.

- They were stabbed—but how?

No Birds Allowed

- This has nothing to do with flying.

- Birds would not last long in a spaceship.

- Weightlessness would be a big problem for them.

A Handful

- The ancients knew of these and clearly identified and tracked six of them.

- The seventh was discovered in 1781 and the eighth in 1846.

- The ninth was discovered in 1930 but disallowed in 2006.

Happy Families

- This is unrelated to wealth, education, or family size.

- A new CEO who inherits a family firm in Japan is often a seasoned and successful corporate executive.

- There is a family tradition in Japan that is very unusual.

The Prank

- The tires were outdoors but not readily visible.

- He was a hoaxer who wanted to cause a stir and did so.

- He set the tires on fire, and did so in an unusual location.

- People jumped to the wrong conclusion

Beat to Death

- The rhythm was not musical.

- The men were in the army.

- No explosions or armaments were involved in their deaths.

- An accident caused them to fall to their deaths.

South Pole Position

- Antarctica is about 98% ice and very few fossils have been found there so that evidence is not conclusive.

- A kind of fuel has been found there, however.

- It is hard and black.

Sales Boom

- This is unrelated to levels of literacy or education.

- This involves a hobby or pastime.

- People participating in this hobby use the pencils to write, but typically they themselves are the only ones to read what they write.

26 Years

- This is not an event that relates to human activity, animals, astronomy, or natural phenomena in general.

- It is to do with the digits of the year.

A Mysterious Woman

- Bank notes with very low serial numbers are highly valued by collectors.
- This woman always manages to get ahold of bank notes with low serial numbers.
- This woman has her picture on the bank notes.

Thanks but No Thanks

- All the houses were originally painted white but many had grown shabby.
- A company offered to paint all the houses blue. The villagers agreed on condition that the houses would be repainted white later.
- The villagers decided to keep the blue color because it had an unforeseen economic benefit.

Guess Your Weight

- The volume of the Earth is 1.1×10^{12} cubic kilometers.
- The density of the Earth is 5.5 grams per cubic centimeter.
- Remember to bear in mind the difference between weight and mass.

Rich Cooking

- The worker was employed by a famous man.
- Written instructions would not have been understood.
- The items later came to have great value.

Delayed Effect

- The deaths were not directly caused by any terrorist activities (such as bombings, shootings, or hijackings).
- The actions of the 9/11 terrorists changed people's attitudes and behaviors in ways that put them in greater danger.
- People changed their travel plans.

Solve for X

- You are looking for a name and an award.
- The X in question is a famous and celebrated prize with a yearly ceremony.
- The X who won is a musician.

Danger in the Garden

- It is not a shovel, trowel, or other sharp or pointed tool.
- It is not a power tool.
- It is a common item used by gardeners when they want to grow and place plants.

Phony Baloney

- He was wrongly blamed by ignorant people for many problems and disasters mentioned on the news.
- The disasters were caused by the weather.
- He was listed in the phone book by a nickname.

The Deadly Bite

- The harm is not caused by biting.
- It is caused by poisons.
- Many teeth contain fillings made from potentially dangerous compounds. How might those compounds be transmitted?

Not Enough

- What we are talking about occurs in nature.

- The Latin for one thousand is *mille*.

- The things that one might expect there to be a thousand of are a means of locomotion.

Par for the Course

- Players who had scored par for the course were shown with a score of 72.

- This player was the only player with the word PAR written after his name. Other players had different letters after their names.

- It was an international golf tournament featuring some of the world's top players.

Does Not Compute

- Millions start with 22 of an item. They later have 32 and later still many have few or none.

- Millions start with 350 of an item. They do not actually lose any but they end up with some 209—some of which may be broken.

- These items occur in nature though you can now get artificial examples.

What Was That?

- It was not a bomb or man-made explosion.

- It happened in the 19th century.

- It happened in Asia.

A Grave Problem

- This location is more remote than the deepest ocean or the South Pole.

- It is not on Earth.

- Nor is it on the moon.

Quo Vadis?

- This has nothing to do with Roman roads, buildings, or agricultural methods.

- It involves something the Romans liked to eat (but the British don't).

- The problem spread slowly across the whole country.

When Push Comes to Shove

- The movement is not caused by the movement of land, continents, or buildings.

- It is a man-made marker.

- It involves ice.

Super-Efficient

- This does not involve the use of a battery or household electricity.

- No combustion is involved.

- This occurs in nature in warm countries.

Country Cousins

- This is not a feature of the land or sea or other geographical aspect.
- It is a man-made orientation that these countries have selected.
- It makes them different from the United States but similar to the U.K.

Unseen

- This common item is not a consumer good.
- It is not man-made.
- Where it is common it can be used as a building material.

Getting Overly Personal

- It is not sent via something that they cut (hair or nails, for example).
- They probably aren't thinking about the fact that they are including their DNA in what they send.
- Whether someone sends it or not may depend on the packaging they're using.

Tee Shot

- His long drive was accurate and well-directed.
- He was not a member of the American team.
- He was a policeman.

Cover Charge

- It was not to protect the table or the food.
- It was not to cover or hide anything.
- It was used for a practical purpose.
- Tablecloths were used before cutlery was used.

Big Al

- Al is not a special or noteworthy person.
- In fact, Al is not a person at all.
- Think of country names. (And focus on thinking of a really big country.)

Look Both Ways

- The members of this group all have held (or currently hold) an important position in society.
- Members include both adult males and females.
- The solution involves a commonly seen set of images of the group.
- The images are most commonly seen in Great Britain.

Poor Reflection

- The criminals deliberately fold in the driver's side-view mirrors on cars.
- Then they wait.
- They are thieves, but they do not steal cars.

Mint Condition

- Milling the edges of coins was introduced in the 17th century in England.
- It was a security measure.
- It reduced criminal activity.

The Hunters

- They track an animal found in Asia, the civet.
- They are not concerned with the animal's hide, habitat, or other animals it interacts with.
- They collect something the animal leaves behind.
- They could collect the same thing elsewhere, but the animal affects the item's flavor.

Swap Shop

- This is not because they have more doctors per capita, or hospitals, or people needing organ donations.
- It is not because of people selling organs (although that does happen).
- It is related to the criminal justice system.

Right This Way

- The extra floor covering is folded in a cupboard.
- The arrow points in a specific direction but it is unrelated to fire exits or other emergency procedures.
- My hotel is in Dubai.

Devious!

- It is a tourist attraction.
- It is in Italy.
- Many people are inclined to visit it.

Stage Fright

- This happened some 200 years after Shakespeare's time.
- The play was performed in other countries, but not in England during this period.
- No religious or political themes were involved.
- The play was not performed because it was considered that its content might cause offense at that particular time.

Sweet!

- The sugar is in solid form.
- It is not used as a foodstuff.
- It is used as a substitute for something.
- It makes action films safer for stuntmen and stuntwomen.

Who Was That Masked Man?

- The man rendered her a service.
- She wanted him to do a quick, clean job.
- She never saw him (or anyone else) again.

Deal or No Deal?

- René was a sportsman who won a suitcase in a bet.
- It led to him getting a nickname.
- He was a snappy dresser.
- The image of his nickname is seen on the global brand that bears his name.

Breaking the Habit

- The plan involved drug users who were already in a treatment program. It improved their success rate.
- The plan made people more likely to voluntarily remain in the program.
- It was more expensive to run the program with the plan (but the improved success rate was worth it).

The Other Leg

- She was physically normal and not suffering from any malady.
- She had not been on vacation recently, nor had she used a sunbed.
- It was to promote her business.

Hand in Glove

- She was neither a competitor nor a spectator.
- She worked at the tournament.
- She had a special skill.
- She brought something to the court and kept something else away.

Detection

- This is based on a true story about the first use of a procedure that is now a common police practice.
- 5,000 men passed the test, so the police did not find their man.
- A chance conversation revealed how the killer had evaded detection.

Most Unlucky

- Hans died in a fall.
- His record was for having the longest of something.
- He had his record-holding item with him at all times.

Born to Be Wild

- He was a normal, healthy human baby.
- There was something unusual about his mother, about the way he was born, and about the place he was born.
- He was born inside a box.

Fulfillment

- It was used for recreation and pleasure.
- It is part of something famous.
- Theoretically it could still be used today, but practically speaking it's impossible for anyone to use it.
- A disaster rendered it unusable.

ANSWERS

Instruction for Destruction

The man went to work on a cold morning. He received a text message from his wife: "Windows frozen." Thinking this referred to her car windows, he texted back, "Pour on some warm water." A little while later he received the reply, "Computer completely dead now."

Blind Dates

They each match the letter they follow—that is, the 2nd (letter) of May is A, the 7th of September is B, the 4th of March is C, and the 1st of December is D.

Fire Escape

She walked out through the front door. Her bedroom was on the ground floor and the kitchen was on the upper floor of her house.

Phew!

The company sold natural gas, which is odorless. By making it smell they helped customers to detect dangerous leaks.

A Cold Reception

The man ran a crematorium. The hapless assistant knew that ashes could be used to melt ice, so he spread the ashes of some bodies over the walkways.

Bad Spelling

The man had been hired to carve weights on gold bars. He was stealing gold from the cavities made by the carving, and was attempting to steal more by using letters instead of numerals, but unfortunately for him, this looked too suspicious and he was caught.

Green-Collar Crime

Steve was found guilty of littering the state highway after a policeman saw him throw an apple core out of his car window.

Take That

Throw a drowning man one end of a rope and he will thank you for a long time; throw him both ends and he will hate you ... but maybe not for long.

Traveling Bags

The man is very rude and frequently loses his temper while checking in for his flights. Some of the airline workers get their revenge on him by quietly misdirecting his luggage to the wrong airport.

The Landslide

The man realized that if the bus had not stopped to let him off, it would have passed the landslide zone and nobody would have been killed.

Unbreakable

Traditionally, at the end of an Italian or Greek wedding a plate is broken. If it fails to break it is considered unlucky.

A Fishy Story

She wanted to buy a house that was currently vacant. After she toured the house with the real estate agent she asked for a few moments alone there. She surreptitiously left the raw fish under the floorboards. She knew that after a while the smell of the decaying fish would put off other buyers, giving her the chance to buy the house for a lower price.

Dog Days

Betty got a dog and named her Ethel. She then shouted and swore loudly at the dog using Ethel's name.

Bungling and Burgling

He had an identical twin brother. Their DNA was the same and the witness couldn't tell them apart. Each blamed the other for the crime so neither could be found guilty beyond a reasonable doubt.

Well-Suited

They are in the final round of a poker championship. Charlie has a black suit—a royal flush in spades. He wins the final hand and the jackpot.

Razed to New Heights

It was the Berlin Wall. As it was being knocked down, so many people came to take away pieces of it as souvenirs that a wall had to be built around it to protect it.

Poor Sed

Sed was born with red hair (or ginger hair, as it called in England, and where those who have it are commonly teased), which began to turn gray when he reached sixty, and became fully gray ten years later.

Lost Sheep

The missing animal was the only ram in the flock and without him the flock could not increase.

Low Visibility

George had his eyes closed.

Changing Clothes

Anna suffered from arthritis and her husband used to help her with anything that needed fastening at the back. She now had to replace her clothes with ones that had front fastenings only.

A Big Leap

The plane was on the runway at Bangda airport in Tibet—the highest airport in the world, at over 15,000 feet above sea level.

Visiting Rights

The couple bought an expensive original painting by a famous painter as an investment. They did not want the risk of keeping it in their home (nor the costly insurance they would have to pay for), so they lent it to a museum.

Lead Astray

Both were teams of criminals. The first gang stole a quantity of lead (the metal, that is).

The Long Bath

Ivan was a fisherman who caught carp in a lake (in Poland, where carp is a popular holiday entree). Carp are bottom feeders, and if you eat them right away they taste muddy. He kept the carp he caught in his bath for a few days to purify them so they would taste better.

Watch Out!

Unlucky bystanders may be killed or injured by falling coconuts.

That's Bazaar

Metal theft is a common problem in England. A church that suffered when lead was stolen from its roof installed a number of beehives on the roof as a deterrent for thieves. This also gave them ability to sell honey at the church bazaar.

Double Trouble

They are baby monitors, used so parents can hear their baby in another room. People also sometimes buy them to monitor their elderly parents.

The Weak Bridge

Having been driven nearly 200 miles, the truck has used up enough fuel to bring the total weight under three tons (a gallon of gasoline weighs over five pounds, and a gallon of diesel weighs over seven), which means it can pass safely over the bridge.

Self-Fulfilling Prophecy

Someone with a heart condition, for instance, might experience sudden death due to the excitement caused by a sudden death playoff.

Commuter Bug

A group of bus drivers won the lottery. They did not show up for work the next Monday so some people (including me) were late for work.

Just Trying to Blend In

The chameleon is unusual in that its eyes can swivel independently of each other, so it has the ability look in two directions at once. In judging whether or not a play is offside, a soccer linesman has to watch the player making the pass, the player receiving the pass, and the last defender. This is very difficult for a human but might be easier for a soccer-savvy chameleon.

Queasy Rider

Carsickness hardly ever affects the driver of the car, so the adult can drive the car.

Bad Move

The man wanted to buy an annuity (an annual pension in return for a lump sum) from an insurance company, and knew that they gave better rates to people who lived in areas where life expectancy was lower. So he moved into the worst neighborhood he could find, secured his annuity, and later moved out.

Less Money, Please!

Workers at the U.S. Bureau of Engraving and Printing, where currency is printed, felt they were being asked to produce too much money. (The same situation could happen at the U.S. Mint, where coins are made.)

Two Jackets Required

He worked in an office with a culture of long hours. When he had finished for the day (at, say, 5:30) he would sneak out of the office but leave one jacket on the back of his chair with a cup of coffee on his desk. People would assume he was still around somewhere in the office.

Bad Habits

The second monk boiled the pea before he put it in his shoe!

Brother or Sister

Each of Kelly's parents had an identical twin and those twins had also married. They had had two children which were genetically equivalent to a brother and sister for Kelly. One of them provided the transplant.

Impressive Identification

John was the only other adult man there. The rest of the spectators were women (probably mothers of the boys who were playing) and children (likely friends or siblings of the players).

On Reflection, It Makes Sense

The man used the car in a filmed advertisement that he wanted to show in various countries around the world. He reversed the film left to right when it was shown in countries where people drive on the other side of the road. The number plate still made sense.

Pen Name

He expected to be signing a lot of autographs, and thought he would save time by not having to lift his pen from the paper to dot the "i."

Dress to Impress

Two thieves set out to rob a fashion store in the middle of the night. They knew there was a risk that they would set off the alarm, which would alert the police—and, in fact, that is exactly what happened. However, they did not flee. They stood stock-still in the shop and pretended to be mannequins; that was why they dressed so smartly.

Shaven Head 1

The woman had four identical quadruplet sons. Even she found it difficult to tell them apart. When they first went to school she shaved the numbers 1, 2, 3, and 4 on their heads to help the teacher identify them.

Shaven Head 2

He had missed the deadline of an important course assignment. He went to his tutor and asked for an extension, claiming that he had been extremely ill and received chemotherapy. He got the extension.

The Reluctant Smoker

The man was on a bus. His destination lay on a long stretch of road between two bus stops. When he lit his cigarette the driver noticed, stopped the bus, and threw the man off—exactly at the point the man wanted.

Going Full Circle

The woman liked to shop for clothes. She had read that some changing room mirrors are doctored to make the customer look slimmer by narrowing the width of the reflection. The woman tested the mirror beforehand by looking at the reflection of the disc. If it appeared as an ellipse rather than a circle, she knew the store was trying to fool her.

Off With Its Head

Your pillow!

That's Cold

The man was driving to Santa Claus Village in the Lapland region of Finland, but he took a wrong turn and wound up near Aalto University's Low Temperature Laboratory instead, a research laboratory where scientist had produced a temperature of less than 100 picokelvins (.0000000001 degrees Celsius above absolute zero), making it the coldest place in the universe. (The lowest observed naturally occurring temperature is in the Boomerang Nebula, which has a temperature of 1 kelvin.)

This Place Is a Zoo

The man was a guide with a bad memory. He wanted to remind himself that the name for two-humped camels, Bactrian camels, starts with a B (which, as a visual reminder, has two humps if you look at it sideways), and that the name for one-humped camels, dromedaries, starts with a D (which has one hump if you look at it sideways).

Bagman

The man is a spy. He mixes the lemon juice and the milk to make invisible ink. When he receives a message written in invisible ink, he heats up the paper with the iron. This makes the writing visible.

100% Chance of Robbery

They went away on vacation and left their cars in the driveway and their house lights set on a timer to turn on and off so that it would not look like they were away. Unluckily for them, it snowed heavily for several days and then stopped snowing. With no footprints on the doorstep, no tracks on the driveway, and the cars obviously stationery it became clear that the house was empty, and burglars pounced.

Getaway Route

You should run in a zigzag pattern (or alternating tight curves). Crocodiles run very fast in a straight line but they are not good at changing direction.

Wedged In

The wedges were meant to increase the range of notes he could play on the piano with each hand. The boy was Chopin, the composer.

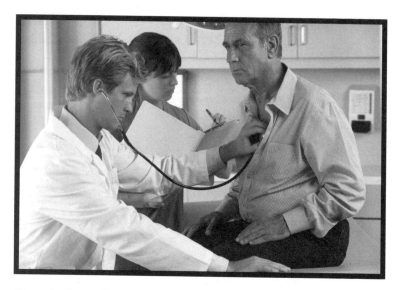

Don't Stand So Close to Me

René-Théophile-Hyacinthe Laennec (1781–1826) was a French physician. He sometimes had to put his ear to a woman's chest to hear her heart. He tried using a roll of paper and found that he could hear the heart much better. He invented the stethoscope in 1816. It significantly improved diagnosis of chest conditions.

Train Fare

Railways in Peru reach altitudes of 10,000 feet. Oxygen canisters are available for travelers who get dizzy.

There's an Awful Lot of Coffee in Brazil

Excess coffee is used to fuel trains. (The aroma must be nice!)

Bright Idea

Matadors usually wear bright red cloaks to cover up the bloodstains they sometimes receive.

Up the Spout

Starbucks Coffee is named after Starbuck, Captain Ahab's first mate in *Moby-Dick*.

Men Only

Walk on the surface of the Moon. (The clue on page 58 refers to Michael Jackson's "moonwalk," naturally.)

Mighty Mini

He was King Kong in the film of the same name. In reality, he was portrayed by small models, the primary one of which was a puppet only eighteen inches tall!

Dangerous Days

They died having been stabbed by falling icicles.

No Birds Allowed

Birds need gravity to swallow. They would choke in space.

A Handful

The number of planets in the solar system. The six planets from Mercury to Saturn (which can all be seen with the naked eye) had all been discovered by the second millennium B.C.E.; Uranus was discovered in 1781, Neptune in 1846, and Pluto in 1930, although since Pluto has recently been reclassified as a dwarf planet, the total number has been reduced to eight.

Happy Families

In Japan it is quite common for families to adopt adults into the family. So a family that has a business and no obvious heir might adopt a young man or woman with good business credentials. The adopted person will change their name and become part of the family.

The Prank

On the morning of April 1, 1974, the residents of Sitka, Alaska, were alarmed to see black smoke rising from the crater of Mount Edgecumbe, the long-dormant volcano that stood nearby. Oliver Bickar, a local practical joker, had flown old tires into the volcano's crater and then lit them. It was one of the most celebrated April Fools' Day hoaxes.

Beat to Death

They were soldiers crossing the Angers Bridge over the Maine river in France. The bridge started to rhythmically oscillate in the wind and the steps of the soldiers may have further increased the resonance, which led to the collapse of the bridge.

South Pole Position

It is almost certain that Antarctica was once situated in the tropics. In 1939, the American explorer Peary found coal seams in rocks less than two hundred miles from the South Pole. These could not have been formed outside the tropics.

Sales Boom

The popularization of sudoku.

26 Years

The year contained no repeated digits.

A Mysterious Woman

Whenever there is a new banknote design printed in the U.K., the Queen is given the first example printed. This has the lowest serial number, which makes it very valuable to banknote collectors.

Thanks but No Thanks

Júzcar, near Málaga in Spain, was transformed in 2011 when it was chosen as the site for the premiere of the 3-D film *The Smurfs*. Sony, which made the film, painted every house in the village blue (though a mushroom-house motif might have been more appropriate), and had promised to return the village to its original color, bright white, as is typical of southern Spain. But local people voted to keep the village blue because it had become a huge tourist attraction.

Guess Your Weight

Weight is the force on a body exerted by the Earth. Since the Earth exerts no force on itself, its weight is zero. Its mass is estimated at 6×10^{24} kilograms.

Rich Cooking

Michelangelo's servants could neither read nor write. As a result, he had to draw shopping lists and menus. These items are now worth a fortune. (One was displayed in a touring museum exhibition in 2009.)

Delayed Effect

Because people were afraid of the threat of plane hijacking (and possibly because of the long waits at security checks) many people chose to take long drives rather than fly. Driving is much more dangerous than flying and, statistically, hundreds of extra deaths must have occurred because of this.

Solve for X

Oscar Hammerstein II won an Oscar for best song in 1941. (Tony awards have been won by multiple Tonys, including playwright Tony Kushner, costume designer Tony Duquette, and scenic designers Tony Walton and Tony Straiges.)

Danger in the Garden

The flowerpot. Falling flowerpots cause a great number of accidents. (Additional accidents are caused by tripping over them, or lifting large, heavy ones incorrectly.)

Phony Baloney

Alfonso Nino was listed in the phone book as "Al Nino," and multiple people called him to complain about the bad weather they were having, which had actually been caused by the effect known as El Niño.

The Deadly Bite

Thanks to the cremation industry, teeth can generate dangerous poisons. Mercury in the fillings of corpses' teeth is vaporized by the intense heat and winds up as atmospheric pollution.

Not Enough

Millipede literally means "a thousand feet" in Latin, but the maximum number of feet a millipede has been found with is about 750.

Par for the Course

The golfer was from Paraguay, the official abbreviation of which is PAR.

Does Not Compute

The answer is ourselves. When we are babies, we have 22 baby teeth, which normally become 32 permanent teeth. Meanwhile, we start out with about 350 bones, which knit together to become 209 adult bones.

What Was That?

The eruption of Krakatoa in 1883 generated the loudest sound in human history—it was heard over 3,000 miles away and caused deafness for anyone unfortunate enough to be within 10 miles. The explosive force of the eruption was about 13,000 times that of the atomic bomb that fell on Hiroshima, and led to the deaths of over 36,000 people. The average temperature around the world fell by about 2 degrees Fahrenheit in the year after the eruption. One small benefit was that the dust in the atmosphere caused many very beautiful sunsets.

A Grave Problem

Eugene Shoemaker had his ashes sent to the moon in a vial. His grave is very remote, but Clyde Tombaugh's ashes are the remotest; a portion of them are aboard *New Horizons*, a spacecraft en route to Pluto.

Quo Vadis?
The Romans introduced snails to the British Isles because they liked to eat them. Snails have multiplied and are now a common garden pest.

When Push Comes to Shove
The marker used to indicate the South Pole has to be moved each year, as the ice in which it is fixed moves about that distance every year. (The Times Square ball drops about 47 yards, in case you were wondering.)

Super-Efficient
The glowworm has the most efficient method of light production—nearly all the energy that contributes to the process is converted to light. (For most light sources, the majority of energy is converted to heat and only around 10% to 20% to light.)

Country Cousins
They all drive on the left-hand side of the road.

Unseen
Snow.

Getting Overly Personal

Their saliva when they lick an envelope or a stamp. In the early days of postage it was feared the system would collapse because people thought it was impolite to send their spittle to each other. (Nowadays, of course, most stamps and many envelopes are self-adhesive, so this doesn't happen every time something is mailed.)

Tee Shot

Rory McIlroy, one of the stars of the European team, got confused by the American time zones and nearly missed his tee time. Pat Rollins, an Illinois policeman and weekend golfer, drove his police car quickly through traffic to escort McIlroy to the course, helping him to make his tee time.

Cover Charge

Tablecloths were originally intended to wipe hands and faces after eating greasy food without knives and forks.

Big Al

Take AL out of AUSTRALIA and you get AUSTRIA.

Look Both Ways

British coins show alternate monarchs facing in opposite directions.

Poor Reflection

When the motorists reach out to adjust their mirrors, the criminals grab the expensive watches from their wrists.

Mint Condition

This was the idea of Isaac Newton when he was Master of the Mint. People used to file the edges off coins and use the metal to make other forged coins. The milled edges prevented this.

The Hunters

Kopi Luwak is the world's most expensive coffee. It is made from the beans of coffee berries that have been eaten by the Asian palm civet and have passed through its digestive tract, having absorbed some enzymes in the process. Indonesian farmers then follow the animals and pick the berries from their droppings, and wash, dry, and roast them, producing a less bitter coffee that retails for hundreds of dollars per pound. (This, at least, is the traditional method of collecting the beans. Because of the coffee's recent popularity, inhumane factory farming of civets is now common, sadly.)

Swap Shop

China has the world's highest rate of capital punishment (though, even so, it is lower than it was a decade ago), and the organs of all executed criminals are recycled to help those waiting for transplants.

Right This Way

Since my hotel room is in the Middle East, the extra floor covering is a prayer mat for Muslims and the arrow on the ceiling shows the direction of Mecca.

Devious!

The Leaning Tower of Pisa now deviates almost exactly four degrees from the vertical, making it world-famous.

Stage Fright

Because of the madness of King George III, *King Lear* was banned in England from 1810 to 1820 (also the period when George III's condition had worsened to the point where his eldest son was appointed as regent). It was felt that it would be indiscreet to stage a play about a mad king when there was a real mad king on the throne.

Sweet!

The fake glass through which stuntmen and stuntwomen jump is made of sugar crystal to prevent injury.

Who Was That Masked Man?

The man was her executioner. It was customary for someone condemned to execution to give a small tip to the executioner. Mary, Queen of Scots did this with the man who wielded the ax.

Deal or No Deal?

In 1923 the French tennis player René Lacoste made a bet with the captain of the French Davis Cup team, who promised him a crocodile-skin suitcase if he won a big match. This was reported by a journalist who nicknamed René Lacoste "the Crocodile." Lacoste had an image of a crocodile embroidered on his blazer. He went on to design a range of tennis clothing all featuring the crocodile; it became the highly popular Lacoste brand.

Breaking the Habit

Stephen T. Higgins, a professor at the University of Vermont, found success with a program that rewarded cocaine abusers who tested negative for drug use with vouchers that could be traded for retail goods and services (and that increased in value with successive negative tests). This proved highly effective at reducing drug use and preventing people from dropping out of treatment.

The Other Leg

Judy Naake is an entrepreneur who made her fortune by launching St. Tropez self-tanning lotion in the U.K. To promote it, she applied it to one of her legs only. When she visited prospective clients she could then show how effective it was. If she had applied it to both legs, people might have thought she had a real tan.

Hand in Glove

The girl works at the Centre Court at Wimbledon. She owns the harrier hawk that deters pigeons from the Centre Court and she brings it along to each match.

Detection

The first time that DNA testing was used in criminal detection was in a murder case in England. In 1987 police in Leicestershire tested all the local men (5,000 of them) in their search for the killer of two girls. No match was found. Since all the men passed the test, it was considered a failure. However, one man was later heard to say that a friend named Colin Pitchfork had paid him to take the test on his behalf. Pitchfork was tested and his DNA matched that found at the crimes. He was convicted and sentenced to life in prison.

Most Unlucky

Hans Steininger held the record for the world's longest beard at 4.5 feet. Unfortunately, one day in 1567 a fire broke out in his town, and, while attempting to distance himself from it, he accidentally tripped on his beard and broke his neck.

Born to Be Wild

As his mother was being buried, a noise was heard from inside her coffin. When the coffin was hurriedly opened, he slipped out of his dead mother's womb, totally healthy.

Fulfillment

It is the swimming pool on the *Titanic*.

About the Authors

Paul Sloane lives in England. He writes and speaks on innovation and lateral thinking in business. He studied engineering at Cambridge University. He and his wife have three daughters and five grandchildren, all of whom get the lateral puzzles treatment. He hosts the Lateral Puzzles Forum at www.lateralpuzzles.com.

Des MacHale lives in Ireland and is Emeritus Professor of Mathematics at University College Cork where he taught for 40 years. He is interested in puzzles of all sorts, particularly ones that show the fun side of mathematics and logic. He and his wife, Anne, have five children who currently live in Sweden, Switzerland, the United States, and Ireland. He is also interested in music, words, jokes, geology, and John Ford's movie *The Quiet Man*. He has written over 60 books on various subjects, with about a dozen more in the pipeline.

Also Available

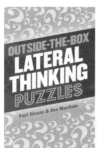

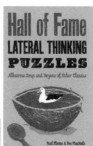